When the *Extraordinary* Invades the Ordinary

An Advent Devotional

Monica Napoli Warren

© Copyright 2020 Monica Napoli Warren

All rights reserved. Permission is granted to copy or reprint portions for any noncommercial use, except they may not be posted online without permission.

Printed by Kindle Direct Publishing
Available from Amazon.com and other retail outlets and bookstores

ISBN 9798693069398

Printed in the United States of America

Because of the dynamic nature of the Internet, any web address or links contained in this book may have changed since publication and may no longer be valid.

Unless otherwise indicated, scripture quotations are from The NASB®, the NEW AMERICAN STANDARD BIBLE(R), Copyright (C) 1960,1962,1963,1968,1971, 1972,1973,1975,1977,1995 by The Lockman Foundation. Used by permission.

For more information about Monica or her other projects, visit www.hijackedjesus.com

To Sarah and Robert Brenner—
dear friends, wise mentors, and faithful servants to King Jesus,
for whom both Claude and I are immeasurably grateful

Introduction

Joyous Advent to you, friends!

Advent is a time of waiting with great expectation. The season rides the waves of traditional sights and sounds, including a retelling of the Christmas story. You know the story…the angel choir led by Gabriel, some shepherds and their flocks, three wise men with camels, Mary (carrying baby Jesus) and Joseph and a donkey, and maybe some Bethlehemites and an innkeeper. Although we know that the Christmas story remains essential to the Gospel, rarely does a retelling evoke the awe-struck astonishment it deserves. Has familiarity robbed us of the miraculous wonder of it all? Are there treasures nestled into the story that have somehow been missed? Is there a way to recapture the unfolding mystery without jumping to baby Jesus in a manger?

Throughout the 1990s, part of my Advent tradition included producing my church's Christmas pageant. I felt it my personal challenge to offer the congregation a unique presentation of the Christmas story, one in which they would "hear it again for the very first time, seeing the shadow of the cross in the cradle." Merging my theater background with my passion for Bible study, each year I dreamed up a unique lens through which to view the Christmas story. Life is comprised of seasons. Seasons pass. My season of producing the annual Christmas pageant passed. But my passion for Bible study continued, with particular fervor for understanding Ancient Near Eastern culture—the Bible's setting and, therefore, imperative for rightly understanding Scripture. This devotion presents the Christmas story with some of what I have learned about the Bible's culture and how it affects the story the Bible is telling. Strands of my theatrical background, as well as my heart's longing to "hear the Christmas story again for the very first time, seeing the shadow of the cross in the cradle," weave their way throughout.

During the four weeks of Advent, we will look at the Christmas story through Luke and Matthew's narrative lenses. Each devotion references two passages of Scripture. The first provides the part of the narrative on which that day's devotion is based. The second supports the narrative, reminding us that the Bible tells a cohesive story. Please, take the time to read both passages. Also, depending on what day of the week Christmas falls in a given year, Christmas Day may arrive before you reach the final devotion on Saturday of Week 4. Please, please, keep reading.

The events surrounding Jesus' conception and birth consist of both the extraordinary and the very ordinary, and they reveal much about the heart, intention, and ways of God. Because of the familiarity of the story, we will move slowly, at times stopping to appreciate and soak in the more obscure details. We will also attempt to bridge the gap created by time and culture, building a set that looks like first century Palestine and seeking to comprehend the mindset of a people longing for liberation but living under oppressive Roman rule. Do not allow familiarity to rob you of fascination. Set what you know aside. Linger in each scene that Scripture paints as the details unravel one at a time. Let the characters come alive; put yourself in their shoes. Stand in awe as ordinary people accept God's invitation to be part of his extraordinary plans. Watch as centuries of promises begin to appear on history's stage in extraordinary ways in the most ordinary places and people. Listen to the story, again, as if for the very first time.

In the end, may we know God more intimately, and in knowing him more, love him more deeply, and cooperate with him more fully in his extraordinary plans.

With great expectation,

Monica

Hope
Week One

Creation, Chaos, and Covenant Hope
Genesis 1; Genesis 3

The word *story* receives a bad rap in the American vernacular. At best, story conjures up memories of children's bedtime books or the last good novel you read as an escape from the busyness and pressures of life. At worst, story reminds you of the lie your five-year-old told or the "fake news" propagated by some agency to manipulate the masses. But people from Eastern cultures view story very differently; to them, story-telling is an essential form of communication. While a story can be fictional, to entertain or teach, a story can also transmit and express the memory of a person (or a people)—bringing to light identity, recalling history, and pointing to the future. Likewise, the Bible—set in an Eastern culture, written by Easterners—tells a story, God's story, a true story, the most extraordinary story ever told. Jesus (from his birth through his ascension) encapsulates the climax of that story. Every climax has a backstory, the events leading up to it, the events into which the climax plays out and finds its meaning. Before we look at Jesus' birth, we must know the story into which he steps. To uncover the backstory of Jesus, we recount a broad overview of the Bible's Old Testament.

In the beginning, God creates. At the center of his creation, God makes humans in his image and gives them a royal vocation, to bear his likeness in the world. However, humans sin. As a result, all creation (man, beast, the earth) writhes and heaves in chaos. But God loves his creation, even amid upheaval and sin. So, he sets in motion the plan to rescue and redeem it by calling and covenanting with Abraham and his descendants (eventually, referred to by many names, including Israel and the Jews). From there, the story takes its reader through the twists and turns and tragedies of the intended rescue vehicle, Israel. At the end of the Old Testament, the intended rescuer has careened into a ditch and is herself in need of rescue. In the ditch, the Jews wait—hoping, longing, and praying—for what the prophets had sketched, what the Psalms had sung, what the ancient promises to the patriarchs had held out in prospect: their God, the rightful king of the world, will return and bring the needed rescue.

Although the *when* remained unknown, and the *how* would come in surprising ways, the Jews knew this salvation would come, because, throughout their history, God had proved himself faithful to his promises.

You are God's beloved created image-bearer, and God is your faithful rescuer. Is there chaos around you or in your life? Remind yourself of God's promises.

An Advent Devotional | 9

Tuesday

All Wrong
Luke 1:5-7; Psalm 68

Luke opens the Christmas story not with Mary, Joseph, and Jesus but another trio of characters: Herod (king of Judea), Zachariah (a Jewish priest), and Elizabeth (Zachariah's wife). And everything seems all wrong from the beginning.

First, Herod is not the rightful king of the Jews, but a murderous puppet-king of Rome, who has proved he would kill even his family members to protect his crown, whether the threats are real or imagined. Herod's tyrannical rule is a grim reminder that the Jews live under Roman occupation as an oppressed people. In Rome's empire, a small group of elites (2-3% of the population) rule, owning the land, controlling production, and consuming 65% of its resources. Everyone else lives in varying degrees of poverty. Rome's army secures and maintains Rome's power and rule. Failure to comply with Rome's laws results in swift and ruthless military action. Politics and religion are not separate, and no one pretends that they are. Rome believes its victory and rule to be divinely sanctioned. In other words, the victory and rule of Rome prove the goddess Roma and the "son of god" Caesar superior to all other local gods, including the Jewish God, Yahweh.

Second, our two righteous, obedient Jews from Aaron's priestly line find themselves childless and too old to hope that will change. In the Bible's world, people viewed childlessness as a disgrace and the result of a defect in the woman. Believing that Yahweh (or some other god, depending who you worshiped) rewarded the obedient and punished the disobedient, any sort of malady was seen as a result of sin. Jesus corrects this misunderstanding about the ways and heart of Yahweh during his ministry. But for now, sympathize with the struggle and the disgrace of Zachariah and Elizabeth, for this is their reality. Furthermore, when people think rescue-mission-participant, the young, robust, and able-bodied come to mind, not the elderly, arthritic, and culturally shamed!

All wrong? Seems that way. But God is apparently neither conventional nor deterred by obstacles. And the powers of earthly kings and their kingdoms neither pose a threat nor prove to be formidable opponents for Yahweh.

Does everything seem all wrong in your life or, maybe, in the world? Make a list of your perceived all wrong obstacles. Then spend some time in prayer, declaring God's superiority over each obstacle.

Extraordinary Ordinary | 10

Fervent Prayers
Luke 1:8-12; Psalm 31

No matter where you live, you probably move through life governed by seasons, whether those seasons be driven by nature, annual holidays, work or school schedules, etc. For first century Jews, their God's temple (Yahweh's temple), with its daily offerings and feasts, created a rhythm for life. Also, if a person wanted to meet with Yahweh, he would go to Yahweh's temple. Therefore, it is fitting that the climactic rescue of the Bible's story begins with events occurring in the Jewish temple. Here, Luke introduces us to more characters in the unfolding Christmas story: a Jewish multitude and an angel named Gabriel.

The incense offering symbolized and expressed the prayers of the Jews, which by this time would have undoubtedly included a petition for Messiah. Twice-daily the incense offering ritual happened this way…when the priest entered the Holy Place with the incense, the people left the temple, waited outside, silently prayed. After placing the incense on the fire, the priest bowed reverently toward the Holy of Holies, retreating slowly backward. Upon emerging from the temple, the priest would stand before the people and say a blessing over them.

Everyday…twice-a-day. Regardless of weather conditions. No matter who sat on Rome's throne. Despite dismal circumstances. The multitudes (not just the appointed priests) gathered at the temple and prayed in hope, in waiting, with certain expectation that God would fulfill his promises. Our need is the same (the intervening rule of God). Our prayer is the same (Please, come!). Yet, all too often, our perseverance is lacking (Forgive us, Lord!).

Tomorrow's devotion focuses on Gabriel's message to the priest Zachariah, but just one quick observation for now. Why do so many depictions of angels portray them as ethereal, docile creatures when (nearly) every biblical recording of an angelic encounter leaves the observer "gripped with fear"? When fully understood in its context, the Christmas story is not a tender tale but a covert, dangerous rescue mission. As such, the Lord of Hosts—one of the names for God, which literally means *Commander of the Heavenly Armies*—sends one of his angelic commanders to deliver a message.

In your waiting, have your faithful prayers waned? If so, reignite your fervent petitions. Meditate on God's power to intervene in your circumstances, remembering that his intervention can come at any time, in any place, in any way, employing anyone.

An Advent Devotional | 11

Thursday

Good news!
Luke 1:13-17, 19; Isaiah 40:1-11

Although the incense offering happened twice-a-day, everyday, it was most likely for old man Zachariah, a once-in-a-lifetime chance to perform this ritual. And on this particular day, the twice-daily incense offering turned out to be anything but routine and ordinary. As Zachariah uttered his "Amen," an angelic warrior filled the room, declaring Zachariah's prayers heard and answered.

> Do not be scared. I bring good news. Those prayers you just prayed while burning the incense—both your personal prayers and the national prayers—have been heard. The world's administration is about to change. Messiah is coming, and your son, John, who Elizabeth will birth, will be the royal herald!

In the New Testament, the Greek word for *good news* (also translated *gospel*) literally means *a reward for bringing good news, a technical term for "news of victory."* In its first century context, *good news* had two meanings: an Isaianic Message and an Imperial Proclamation. Both meanings apply here. Isaianic Message refers to the Old Testament prophet, Isaiah, since he referred to Yahweh's coming intervention in the affairs of human history, to free Israel from her exile and bring salvation, as *good news*. In other words, it is the *good news* about Messiah. Imperial Proclamation refers to the announcement of the birth or accession of an emperor. The following brief history lesson serves as a helpful illustration of *good news* as an Imperial Proclamation in the context of the Roman world.

> On September 2, 31 BC, Octavian defeated Mark Antony, ending years of civil war in Rome. Heralds dispersed across Rome announcing, "Good news! Octavian is the victorious and reigning king. He has brought peace, justice, and prosperity to the world!" Beginning with Octavian (better known as Caesar Augustus), the Roman emperors regularly used the words *good news* to describe both what they had already achieved and what life would now be like as a result.

Read the first century meanings of *good news* into Luke's narrative. Most certainly, Zachariah would have heard Gabriel's announcement in that way.

Jesus came to establish a new regime—a new king, with a new way of ruling, creating new citizens who form new communities. How would living out of this truth impact your relationship with Jesus and others?

Friday

Yikes! Wrong Question
Luke 1:18-22a; Isaiah 40:12-31

Relish the raw, honest humanity portrayed throughout the Bible's story. The writers do not sugarcoat the characters, flawed vessels who partner with God despite themselves. Fully functioning man enters the temple to perform an ordinary daily ritual. Foreboding angel interrupts ritual to give stunning, extraordinary good news. Man asks the wrong question. Angel strikes man mute until the angel's bit of good news comes to pass. Mute man exits the temple.

How should one respond to extraordinarily great news such as that which Gabriel delivered to Zachariah? Apparently, not the way Zachariah did. Zachariah did not ask how the impossible was possible. He questioned the promise's reliability, asking "How do I know you speak the truth?" Could it be despite the years Zachariah walked blamelessly before God—outwardly doing the right things, keeping the Law—he had relied on his circumstances as the barometer of God's love and goodness toward him and, as a result, found God wanting?

As already mentioned, childlessness was a disgrace, and women bore the responsibility for a couple's childless status. In light of this, marriage contracts permitted two things if a wife failed to deliver a child within two years: a man could divorce his wife or a woman could provide a maidservant by which her husband could have a child. Zachariah demanded neither, not casting Elizabeth aside via divorce, nor siring a child by a maidservant. To live honorably before God and with his wife, Zachariah refused to give in to what his culture determined "his rights." Furthermore, Zachariah knew the stories within Israel's history of God opening barren wombs. Why had God not moved on behalf of him and Elizabeth? God had let Zachariah down, depriving Zachariah of a child and allowing him and Elizabeth to endure the shame of childlessness all these years. Why or how or should Zachariah trust God now? Raw, honest humanity. (Perhaps you and I can relate.)

Have you felt that you have "done the right things" only to have life deal unfairly with you? Have you judged God's heart toward you based on your circumstances? Let the sweetness of God toward Zachariah encourage you. Zachariah may have lost hope and become jaded. But God loved Zachariah and did not allow Zachariah's' doubt or wrong ideas about him to deprive Zachariah of his love or disqualify Zachariah from being part of his extraordinary plans.

An Advent Devotional | 13

Saturday

It Has Begun
Luke 1:21-25; Malachi 4

Can you just imagine the scene outside the temple that day? Come. Kneel with me there, silently, in prayer. You finish your usual prayers, and since the priest has not reappeared, you throw in a few more prayers. Still no priest, you sheepishly glance around and notice others starting to look up, too. I nudge you, "This seems to be taking longer than usual." You nod. We hear whispers of similar sentiments. Suddenly, Zachariah appears. Phew! Along with everyone else, we anticipate Zachariah's verbal blessing over us. Instead, before us stands a wide-eyed man who gestures wildly, unable to speak. This is highly unusual… extraordinary even.

Luke only tells his readers that the people realized Zachariah had seen a vision. Did the people know the vision pertained to the promised Messiah? Did the people depart the temple area with great expectation? Or in great confusion? Or both? Zachariah, along with the other priests, finished his duties before returning home to relay the extraordinary news to Elizabeth. Again, Luke's lack of narration leaves his readers to speculate and wonder. Oh, to have been a fly on the wall at Zachariah's house! All we know is, once Elizabeth becomes pregnant, she tucks herself away for five months, basking in the joy of pregnancy and the love and goodness God has shown her.

Zachariah and Elizabeth's life provides a powerful reminder. Not every perceived *disgrace*—something that is seemingly wrong in someone's life—is a result of something that person did wrong. And, God is working out an unseen puzzle, which will result in our good and his glory.

The dead dreams of an old priest and his barren, aged wife intersect with the plans of God, bringing life into a dead womb and setting into motion the plan for ultimate redemption. An old man finally fathers a child, a son. A barren woman finds deliverance from social disgrace. An oppressed people hear the first notes of hope's song. A world groaning under the weight of sin and death begins to awaken to the first rays of light piercing the darkness, all because God longs to show mercy and keeps his covenants and promises. But understand, the fulfillment of God's promises flowering before us will be wrought with danger, with many unexpected and surprising twists and turns.

Reflecting on the way God brings the news of Messiah's forerunner, and who God chooses to parent the Messiah's forerunner, what do you observe about God's character?

Faith

Week Two

Act I Scene 2
Luke 1:26a; Psalm 103

If we read the Christmas story in the form of a theatrical drama, Zachariah and Gabriel's scene might be Act 1 Scene 1, and Luke 1:26a could be Act 1 Scene 2. As such, Act 1 Scene 2 rarely receives any attention at all. But, taking not a few artistic liberties, we can infer the scene scripted as the opening words of Luke 1:26 and in conjunction with Luke 1:19. The scene takes place in the heavenly throne room. The cast features God (Father, Son, Spirit) and Gabriel. Gabriel has just returned from his deployment to Jerusalem, where he delivered big news to the elderly priest, Zachariah, as he stood burning the incense.

Gabriel enters, bowing before his maker and king. Then, a joyous reunion of friends ensues with hugs all around! God debriefs Gabriel concerning the Jerusalem deployment, and all agree Gabriel handled Zachariah's "doubt question" nicely. God presents Gabriel with an envelope containing the details of his next deployment, to be conducted precisely six months after his appearance to Zachariah. Upon reading the mission details, Gabriel sits down, stunned. He looks wide-eyed at each member of the Trinity. With all due respect, in complete willingness to execute the mission as instructed, and with unwavering confidence in God's goodness and plans, the seasoned veteran's earnest concerns spill out: "God, you will begin your ascent to the throne as a baby? You will depend completely on the Image Bearers for all of your needs, your safety? But what about how the Image Bearers have continuously spoiled creation, both themselves and the world around them? To trust them with such a gift, the Son, is…well…extraordinarily dangerous! And I can hardly bear the thought of seeing you as a helpless baby." Knowing the loyalty of his faithful servant, God the Father gently acknowledges Gabriel's concerns. The mission *is* dangerous. Everything *is* at stake. But *love* compels action…self-sacrificial, self-emptying action.

Of course, Gabriel will go and faithfully execute the plan. The scene ends as it opens—warm hugs between intimate friends. This new news has brought reason for even more joy, although somewhat tempered by the sobering realities of the mission's danger. Then, Gabriel bows to his maker and king and exits the room.

Oh, the depths Love has gone to rescue us!

Ponder the height, depth, length, and breadth of a love that would risk so much to rescue you.

Tuesday

Ordinary Mary
Luke 1:26b-27; 1 Samuel 16:1-13

Six months after yesterday's events, armed with his message, Gabriel visits Mary, and once again the ordinary collides with the extraordinary in our unfolding Christmas story.

An ordinary Jewish girl of the ordinary age to become betrothed, Mary is betrothed to an ordinary man named Joseph in an ordinary Jewish village called Nazareth. Like all other respectable ordinary girls of Mary's age and situation, she remains a virgin. And although Luke does not disclose Mary's activity when Gabriel interrupts her day, it is safe to assume Mary is performing one of her everyday, ordinary tasks.

Considering Mary's ordinary status, she is most likely between the ages of twelve and fourteen, with Joseph being older, perhaps seventeen to twenty. Joseph and Mary are betrothed. This means that sometime within the last year, representatives of Mary and Joseph—most likely their parents—made arrangements for their marriage. The parents took oaths and exchanged gifts. Then, everyone enjoyed a celebration feast, marking this part of the marriage process. It may be tempting to think of Joseph and Mary as being engaged, but please do not. While both betrothal and engagement represent a mutual promise for future marriage, the former more closely resembles marriage, requiring a certificate of divorce to terminate.

Since the betrothal feast, Mary has been living in her parents' home, while Joseph has been at his father's house, preparing a space for him and Mary to live. Any day now, Joseph will come for Mary in a grand procession—with family, friends, flowers, musicians, singing, and dancing. The great procession will move Mary from her house and meander through the streets of Nazareth until they arrive at Joseph's house. There, with family and friends waiting outside, Mary and Joseph will consummate their marriage. Afterward, the bloodstained garment, proving Mary a virgin, will be put out the window of the room, and the seven days of feasting and partying will commence! (Note: In light of betrothal and marriage customs, a pregnancy at the present point in Mary and Joseph's relationship would result in presumed adultery.)

God still calls ordinary people in the midst of living ordinary lives. What might this reveal about God's character?

Wednesday

Blessed
Luke 1:28-30; Genesis 12:1-9

Suddenly, during Mary's ordinary, the extraordinary occurs. An angel appears, calling Mary blessed, declaring the Lord is with her.

What exactly does it mean when the Bible speaks of someone being blessed? God's presence and activity in a person's life renders a person blessed. That life might be messy and even full of pain. But God is present, and his presence imbues blessing. Furthermore, to be blessed of God positions a person as a conduit through whom others experience God's blessing. In other words, we are blessed to be a blessing to others—not to sit in a pool of blessings but to surrender as a passage for blessings. Consider the first person in the biblical record to whom God extends blessing, Abraham. God promises, "I will bless you…and you shall be a blessing" (Genesis 12:2).

Like Abraham before her, God's active presence in Mary's life makes her a channel through whom God's blessings flow to the world. Yet, the extraordinary words that Mary receives, the ramifications of her blessedness, propel Mary into extraordinary danger and uncertainty (ushering in a list of impossibilities we will consider tomorrow).

Luke, the author of the Gospel of Luke, was not one of the original twelve disciples of Jesus, but a Gentile who traveled with Paul years after Jesus' ascension. According to his introduction, Luke carefully investigated the stories of Jesus, interviewing eyewitnesses, to write his Gospel. What must it have been like to interview Jesus' mother, to hear about Jesus (his birth, life, ministry, death, resurrection, ascension) from his mother's perspective? Luke presumably interviewed Mary, granting his readers Mary's private, internal responses at three points in the Christmas story. Here, Luke tells readers that Gabriel's opening words throw Mary into confusion and distress. (The Greek word indicates strong, intense emotion.) Our observation from last week about people encountering angels holds true. No wonder Gabriel must immediately tell Mary not to be afraid. He delivers calming and comforting words before revealing the extraordinary news.

How have you experienced the blessings of God? Are you sitting in a pool of blessings, or are you surrendered as a passage for blessing others? How can you share God's blessings with someone else this week?

An Advent Devotional | 19

Thursday

Extraordinary Purpose
Luke 1:31-33; Psalm 8

Extraordinary news! The time of fulfillment for God's promises of salvation has come, and God has chosen to impregnate ordinary Mary with his purposes. Mary will become pregnant and give birth to a son to be named Jesus. Jesus is the promised one, the very Son of God, who will sit on David's throne forever.

At the beginning of God's story, God created the world and, out of the earth's dust, made humans *in our image and according to our likeness* (Genesis 1:26). *Image* signifies our reasoning abilities, our free will, our sense of moral responsibility, basically everything that sets us apart from the animal creation and makes us persons. God endows every human with his *image*. Bearing God's *image*, humans are God's offspring, his kin, and as such, possess the capacity to commune and fellowship with God and to know God. On the other hand, *likeness* is a goal, an aim, something we acquire in degrees. If we make proper use of communion with God, we become *like* God, obtaining divine *likeness*. Humans never lose *image*, but *likeness* depends on choices. Sin destroys *likeness*. Think of it this way: with whom (or what) we spend time is that which we worship. With whom (or what) we spend time shapes and forms us and our actions. In other words, we become *like* what we worship. We are created in the *image* of God and destined to grow into the *likeness* of God through fellowship with him. Given the royal task of ruling, humans work as stewards, partnering with God in his creation. This is what it means to be truly human, as God intended at creation.

Behind Mary's extraordinary news is a stunning and extraordinary reality about God. Although God has always existed as perfect and good and utterly capable of doing all things himself, he chooses to impregnate ordinary people with his purposes—inviting them to partner with him, entrusting them to guard and protect and nurture and work those purposes to their fullness. Even though humans sin, thus destroying *likeness* in varying degrees, God never rescinds their royal vocation. He is still searching the earth for men and women who worship him, men and women who will say "yes" to being impregnated with his extraordinary plans and purposes.

Take time to reflect on what shapes and forms your actions. In other words, who (or what) do you worship? Into whose (or what) likeness are you growing?

Friday

May It Be…Despite Impossibilities
Luke 1:34-38; Isaiah 46:3-13

Do the purposes into which God has invited you seem impossible? Then you would be in good company with Mary. What are some "impossibilities" Mary faces?

- Becoming the first and only pregnant virgin
- Since Mary is betrothed to Joseph, Mary would be presumed an adulteress. (Remember, do not think engagement. Betrothal is more like unconsummated marriage.) According to the Law of Moses, adultery is a sin punishable by death. Although the penalty was rarely enforced, in adherence to present cultural expectations, Joseph would presumably divorce Mary and expose her to shame.
- Living in a shame-honor culture—where a person does everything to avoid shame and to gain honor—what man would ever marry Mary in her disgrace? Would her family even stand by her?
- Finally, with no husband and marked by shame, Mary faces a life of dishonor and uncertainty, with no way to support herself and her son.

In light of these "impossibilities" (creating very real dangers for Mary and her baby), it is extraordinary that Mary does not ask for time to think about accepting the invitation into God's plans and purposes. But Gabriel has given Mary the secret to overcoming and enduring the impossibilities she faces…Holy Spirit. Mary knows the stories of old: how the Spirit of God hovered over the waters at creation, how he strengthened the judges to liberate Israel from her oppressors, and how he spoke through the mouths of prophets to declare the word of the Lord. Now God's Spirit will be upon Mary as an active participant in God's rescue mission.

Behind Luke's brief recount of Mary's "yes" is a giant-sized declaration of faith: "I am—above all else that I am, more than everything else that defines me—the servant of the one true God. More than my desire to avoid danger and avert fear—at the expense of my understanding, my future hopes and dreams, my personal relationships, my reputation and honor, and even my life—let the one true God's will be done, and his kingdom come, in and through me." (Luke 1:38, my paraphrase)

Would you accept God's invitation as readily as Mary with a bold declaration, "May it be…despite the impossibilities"?

Saturday

Mary & Elizabeth
Luke 1:39-56; Psalm 34

Again, envision Mary. But this time, picture Mary after her angelic visit. The room is still. Quiet. The chair in the corner? Still there. The half-swept floor? Still only half-swept. Mary looks down at her dress. Same dress, not even glittery. Mary slowly moves her hands—which do not glow with some halo effect—placing them across her abdomen. Nothing...flat...small. Same as before. The voices of doubt begin to taunt. "You have such a dramatic and vivid imagination, Mary! You do hear how impossible all this sounds, Mary? And even if it is time for Messiah, why would God choose you, ordinary Mary? Perhaps you are going mad, Mary." Suddenly, Mary remembers something the angel said about dear, old, barren cousin Elizabeth. Elizabeth is now six months pregnant. Mary must go to her. Elizabeth will be tangible proof to silence the voices of doubt. With haste, Mary packs a bag.

Mary travels roughly 100 miles to reach Judea's hill country, arriving at the home of her cousin. Before Mary can raise her hand to knock on the door, Elizabeth swings open the door, her smile indescribably bright. Immediately, Mary fixes on Elizabeth's belly...round, bulging, brimming with life. Tears cascade down the cheeks of both women as they fall into one another's embrace.

Can you even imagine the conversations that took place over the next three months? Yes, being invited into this extraordinary plan of God was an honor and a privilege beyond Mary's wildest dreams. But the journey would be difficult. In those early months, God gifted a heart-friend for Mary, her older cousin. Elizabeth would believe every word of Mary's story, fan the flames of her faith, quiet her fears, speak prophetically into her circumstances, and stand by her.

Gaze upon the Middle Eastern trio—Zachariah, Elizabeth, and Mary—against their first century Ancient Near Eastern backdrop. Now, remove the backdrop and change their clothes, maybe darken the color of Zachariah's skin, lighten Elizabeth's pigmentation, and give Mary a yellow hue. These people could be anyone, from any place, at any time in history—any beautiful humans, created in the image of God, created to partner with God.

Who has God brought alongside you to help carry the plans and purposes he has put in you?

Extraordinary Ordinary | 22

Joy

Week Three

Birth of John
Luke 1:57-80; Psalm 106

Remember back to the first week of Advent, when Gabriel intersected Zachariah in the temple while presenting the incense offering. Had things gone according to the ordinary, every-day, twice-a-day incense offering, Zachariah would have emerged from the temple, stood on the front steps, faced the waiting crowd, and spoken a blessing over the people. However, no blessing flowed from the mouth of the priest who had just burned the incense. Instead the people watched a miming priest and surmised the priest had seen a vision.

Fast forward nine months...for Zachariah, nine months of muteness. Elizabeth did indeed become pregnant and give birth to a son. On circumcision day for the miracle baby, Elizabeth announces that the baby's name shall be John. Neighbors and relatives look to Zachariah to set Elizabeth straight, since no one in the family bears the name John. Zachariah writes upon a tablet, "His name is John." With that, his tongue is loosed, and the blessing withheld nine months ago on the temple steps bursts forth in Judea's hill country. The blessing declares that God is acting now to fulfill his promises of salvation.

Sin caused exile and slavery. Therefore, what was needed was a new exodus, an exodus of salvation that would deal with sin. Behind the phrase used to describe this salvation—*sins will be forgiven*—lay several expectations. These expectations include:

- The return of Creator God to live among his people and to rule as king.
- The Spirit will come; his anointing will give Messiah authority to act.
- As a result, a new world order, a new regime (the kingdom of God), will be established, its citizens hailing from every tribe and every nation.
- Life under this new regime will mean forgiveness and healing, resulting in freedom and peace and ushering in a time of great joy and feasting.
- Death will be abolished and the dead bodily resurrected.

Who can forgive sins? Who can free creation from the bonds of slavery? Who can restore creation and the divine vocation? None other than God himself through Israel's anointed one, Messiah.

Can you hear the hope in Zachariah's prophetic blessing? How does understanding the Jewish hope of salvation give you an increased appreciation of what Jesus has done through his coming?

An Advent Devotional | 25

Tuesday

Sit with Joseph
Matthew 1:18; Psalm 23

To peer into the next scene of our story, we must leave Luke and spend a little time with Matthew.

Like Mary, Joseph is ordinary. An ordinary young man (age seventeen to twenty), he labors in an ordinary trade (a craftsman) and lives in an ordinary small Jewish village (Nazareth). Joseph works on what ordinary young Jewish men his age ordinarily work on when betrothed to a young woman, preparing a place in his father's house for the soon-to-come day when he will bring Mary home to consummate their marriage and begin an ordinary life together. Surely, like an ordinary young man, Joseph can hardly wait for that soon-to-come day.

But Mary has just returned from a three month visit with her cousin, and she has given Joseph some extraordinary news, so EXTRA-ordinary, it is unbelievable. Mary is pregnant, and her virgin-story-explanation is, frankly, impossible. While news that Joseph's betrothed has committed adultery is barely conceivable, it seems like the reality.

What will Joseph do?

Do not rush to the conclusion. Do not insert the end you know. Just sit with Joseph, there, on verse 18, in the almost-finished-room he has been building for Mary and himself. Feel Joseph's devastation and anger. Suffer alongside him the weight of betrayal and shame. Watch with him as he sees his dreams slip away. Hear him recite the Law of Moses, for as an ordinary Jew, he knows it by heart. Listen as he recalls Scripture, perhaps even the words of the prophet Micah by which he has tried to live, *…what does the Lord require of you, but to do justice, to love kindness, to walk humbly with your God.* Do not turn away when he lets out a guttural cry of anguish. Stay with him, there, on verse 18.

In addition to Joseph's struggle, recall the "impossibilities" listed in last Friday's devotion (especially regarding the Law's penalty for committing adultery, Mary's presumed sin, as well as the shame-honor culture in which our story takes place). Can you feel the social, relational, and emotional tension between Joseph and Mary, between their families?

What would you do, what do you do, when faced with overwhelming disappointment, pain, and/or anger?

Wednesday

Just Joseph
Matthew 1:19; Isaiah 42:1-13

Joseph moves from verse 18 (Matthew 1:18); thus, so shall we, but only to verse 19. Joseph has decided what to do about Mary, his betrothed who has shamefully turned up pregnant, and he is not the father of the child she carries. Many people dwell on Mary's obedience in God's plans. However, the choice of Joseph as Jesus' earthly father seems just as deliberate and essential as the choice of Mary to be Jesus' mother. Joseph's intended action recorded in verse 19 gives us a glimpse of his honorable character. Resist the temptation to recall the truth about Mary and her pregnancy or about what comes next in verse 20. Stay with Joseph, with what he presently knows, with only the information at hand.

Matthew describes Joseph as being a *just* man. The word *just* (translated *righteous* in some versions) describes both the man, Joseph, and his actions, how he chooses to respond to an injustice. Not wanting to disgrace Mary further, Joseph has determined to look deeper than the letter of the Law of Moses (the penalty for adultery), opting to divorce Mary quietly. By rejecting the cultural norm to expose her publicly, Joseph forgoes retribution (retributive justice that works on the premise, "you hurt me; so I will hurt you"). Furthermore, he will suffer penalty for his merciful actions. According to betrothal laws, if Joseph divorces Mary "without cause," he must pay a literal fee. He will also shoulder the reputation of a man who divorced his betrothed "without cause."

Joseph acts in the *likeness* of God, emulating both the character of God and the justice of God, searching for a form of restorative justice. Isaiah's prophetic words about the suffering servant to come give us a glimpse of how restorative justice works and how it deals with those who hurt. *A bruised reed he will not break, and a dimly burning wick he will not quench; he will faithfully bring forth justice* (Isaiah 42:3). At significant cost to himself, Joseph chooses compassion and mercy over the letter of the Law. Perhaps Joseph recognizes that sin strips us naked. (Surely, Mary feels exposed and exhausted.) Perhaps Joseph knows that hurting people hurt people. (Some pain in Mary must have driven her to unfaithfulness.) Perhaps Joseph understands that sin makes us a captive of God's enemy. (The consequences of Mary's actions, for Mary, will result in far more than divorce.)

Who has sinned against you? What might it look like to respond to that person, to that situation, in the likeness of God?

Change of Plans
Matthew 1:20-21; Isaiah 9:1-7

Having made the painful decision to divorce Mary quietly—choosing compassion and mercy over the letter of the Law, at great cost to himself—Joseph seeks solace in sleep. And that is when it happens. During ordinary sleep, Joseph comes face-to-face with the extraordinary, and everything changes. An angel visits Joseph in a dream saying, "Don't be afraid to marry Mary. What you believed inconceivable (Mary committing adultery) has not happened, but rather the impossible has happened. The baby in Mary's womb is the Son of God, the long-awaited Messiah."

Translation: Hey, Joseph! You know those dreams you watched walk away the other day when you heard Mary's impossible news? They just walked back into the room with balloons and confetti. Sure, this situation will raise more than a few eyebrows. Yes, people will talk and cast shaming glances. But you are invited to be part of God's plans. Joseph, you best get dressed. You are going to be the step-father, the earthly dad, to Messiah.

The angel's news invites Joseph to join Mary in the extraordinary plans of God. But the angel delivers more than mere instructive information. The message reflects tender care for Joseph. Listen to the words of verse 21:

Joseph, son of David... not Joseph, son of Alpheus, or Bartholomew's son Joseph, but you, Joseph, son of David, intentionally chosen

*Don't be afraid to take Mary as your wife...*the words are gentle, speaking to Joseph's broken, betrayed, and fearful heart, resurrecting a dead dream

For that which has been conceived in her is of the Holy Spirit... the message, among other things, reconciles a broken relationship, restores trust between a husband and his wife, blows away the fog and confusion, and reveals the truth of the circumstances

Sometimes God calls people to hard things, but God never lacks compassion for people in the hard things. Furthermore, God never asks us to do something that he himself is not already doing. In the dream, the angel delivers just what Joseph needs to boldly step into his role in God's unfolding plans.

How have you experienced God's compassion while working in God's plans, especially in difficult seasons?

Friday

Joseph Marries Mary
Matthew 1:24-25; Psalm 84

So, Joseph marries Mary. In light of the culture in which the Christmas story takes place (a shame-honor culture where a person does everything to avoid shame and defend honor), by marrying Mary under these circumstances, would Joseph be defending Mary's honor? Or joining Mary in her shame? Or maybe both?

Would you? Could you? Knowingly, willingly, step into a "shameful" situation to walk alongside someone else? Deliberately placing yourself on the side of the outcast, the marginalized, or even the sinner? Knowing that the whispers and antipathy aimed at them would also be projected onto you? Joseph enters into Mary's presumed shame. (Jesus will do the same for countless others.)

Do not toss the question aside too quickly; let it turn in your thoughts today. American Christians do not live in a shame-honor culture. However, in our success-driven culture, dreams about being invited into the plans of God—about doing big things for God and his kingdom—are usually accompanied by visions of honor and prestige, maybe even notoriety and monetary gain, counting success in numbers (whether that be the number of people who follow us on social media, buy our books, sit in our pews, attend our Bible studies, etc.). But as we enter Mary and Joseph's context, do we see these familiar ideas of "doing big things for God"? Thinking back to Zachariah and Elizabeth, they endured a lifetime of public disgrace because of Elizabeth's barrenness. But Elizabeth's barrenness proved fertile soil for bearing God's plan, for birthing and raising the Messiah's herald, John.

Jewish teachers believed men should marry young so as not to succumb to sexual temptation. Although the Gospel writers withhold information as to the relational dynamics between Joseph and Mary as husband and wife, in verse 25 Matthew tells his readers that Joseph keeps Mary a virgin until she gives birth. Joseph denies himself, his "rights" and his desires, to play his part in God's bigger story—*Behold, a virgin shall conceive, and bear a son...* (Isaiah 7:14). As before, we catch glimpses of a man who whole-heartedly participates in the mission and call of his life to raise Jesus as his son.

Sometimes partnering with God means denying our own desires, laying down our plans. What have you denied, or laid down, to partner with God? Has God ever invited you to walk alongside someone cloaked in shame?

Saturday
Clearing the Stage
Luke 2:1-6; Micah 5:2-5a

With Christmas nearing, we turn our gaze back to Luke for the birth of Jesus. Christmas pageants usually portray the birth of Jesus something like this: Caesar Augustus orders a census. Joseph journeys to his hometown of Bethlehem to be counted. Mary, his very pregnant wife, travels alongside him, riding on a donkey. Upon arrival in Bethlehem, Mary goes into labor. Joseph can find no room in the inn. Thankfully, the innkeeper shows compassion, allowing the young couple the use of his stable. Among the livestock, Mary gives birth, and she lays the baby Jesus in a manger. Well, sort of correct, but not exactly.

About 200 years after the birth of Jesus, an anonymous author wrote *The Protevangelium of James*. This story gives numerous recognizable, but wholly imaginative, details surrounding Jesus' birth, many of which expose the author's unfamiliarity with Jewish tradition and Palestinian geography. Even though early biblical scholars attacked the novel, and the average Christian has never heard of it, its content continues to unconsciously influence how we envision the events surrounding Jesus' birth.

Let us take a fresh look at the humble beauty of Jesus' birth. Clear the stage of the usual Christmas pageant's cast and construction. Allow Luke's text and Ancient Near Eastern cultural context to reset the stage and reorder the cast.

Thus, the story opens…Caesar Augustus demands a census, and each must register in his hometown. Joseph, being from King David's family, must travel to Bethlehem. Okay. So far, so good. Our familiar version of Jesus' birth matches the story narrated by Luke. But our first adjustment has arrived. Look closely at Luke 2:6. *And it came about, while Mary and Joseph were in Bethlehem, the days were completed for her to give birth.* The text does not indicate an immediate birth upon arrival, but rather a pregnancy that reaches full term while Joseph and Mary are in Bethlehem.

So, no knocking frantically, going from inn to inn? Because Mary's contractions are worsening, as the young couple nears Bethlehem? No, not according to Luke.

Knowing God is a growing relationship. Growing in knowing sometimes requires a change of mind, especially when we discover that preconceived ideas are wrong. When was the last time you changed your mind about God? What changed, and why?

Peace

Week Four

No Room in the Inn but Welcomed Anyway
Luke 2:7; Deuteronomy 10:12-22

Moving on to Luke 2:7, we uncover our next adjustment to transform our traditional twenty-first century Western nativity scene back into a first century Ancient Near Eastern nativity scene. To do this, we must go on a parade of homes, specifically into simple village homes. These houses have only two rooms—the main room and a guest room. The name for this guest room is the actual meaning of the Greek word translated *inn* in verse 7. This room is used exclusively by guests. The main room divides into two areas, a family room where the entire family lives (sleeping, cooking, eating) and a stable, located at the end and next to the door. Heavy timbers, or a drop in the floor's level, divide the family living area and the stable area, where animals spend their nights. Larger animals eat from feeding troughs, called mangers, carved into the floor at the edge of the family room nearest the stable.

Upon arriving in Bethlehem, Joseph was not turned away from an over-booked motel. In fact, he was not turned away at all. How can we be sure? Because of what we know about first century Ancient Near Eastern culture, specifically concerning hospitality and honor. Consider these facts. Establishments that even remotely resemble a modern-day "inn" were rare in the Ancient Near East. Travelers found lodging via the hospitality of villagers. People considered showing hospitality not only a person's duty, but an honor. Therefore, not showing appropriate hospitality was shameful. Joseph had returned to the village of his origin, and he descended from the royal line. These elements would neither be forgotten nor overlooked in the culture, and it meant most homes would be open to Joseph. Furthermore, the community cared for pregnant women and assisted them during a baby's birth. To neglect a pregnant woman or a woman in labor would be shameful. Finally, had Joseph been denied hospitality in Bethlehem, Mary's relatives (Zachariah and Elizabeth) lived nearby in the hill country of Judea. (Bethlehem is located in Judea.) It would have been a blight on Joseph's honor for him to not seek shelter with Zachariah and Elizabeth in the days between their Bethlehem arrival and Mary's pregnancy reaching term.

Joining Luke's text with the culture, we uncover that although there is no room in the *inn*, with the guest room already occupied, a local Bethlehemite family welcomes Joseph and his pregnant wife anyway. (Note: Luke never mentions a stable.)

God cares about our hospitality. Find a way to practice hospitality this week.

An Advent Devotional | 33

Tuesday

The Incarnation
Luke 2:1-7; Isaiah 53

The Christmas pageant plot, according to Luke's first century narrative, reads something like this: Caesar Augustus orders a census. Taking Mary along (who may or may not have ridden a donkey), Joseph travels to Bethlehem to register for the census. Almost assuredly, Bethlehem bulges at its seams, and each home, per the rules of Ancient Near Eastern hospitality, hosts weary travelers. The guest room (*inn*) of the home in which Mary and Joseph stay is occupied. Despite this, the homeowner, in keeping with custom and honor, welcomes the young couple from Nazareth into his home. While in Bethlehem, the time comes for Mary to give birth. Mary wraps her newborn son in swaddling clothes and lays him in one of the mangers carved into the family room floor.

Surely, those who witnessed Jesus' birth in a peasant family's small home saw little evidence that this boy was anything but ordinary. Birth pains begin. A mother-to-be struggles through each contraction while the other women tend to her needs, sympathizing with her pain, encouraging her to stay focused. The men wait outside for word. Push hard. Dig deep. An infant cries. Spread the news! Mother and child emerge safely through labor and delivery. The boy appears healthy. But, he is born into poverty. Life is hard for Jews living under Roman oppression. Nothing indicates that something out of the ordinary has taken place, much less something extraordinary, such as a king has entered the room.

Until…a knock at the door. But that is getting ahead of the story. Remain here and contemplate the Incarnation, God becoming human, which lays at the heart of God's redemptive agenda.

While Jesus' conception boasts the extraordinary, the events surrounding his birth take place as an ordinary human experience. Recall the beginning of the Bible's story. Creation derailed because humans sinned, missing the mark of what it means to be truly human. By becoming human—experiencing life as fully human from birth to death—Jesus redeems our humanity, making beautiful what it means to be human.

Spend at least 15 minutes meditating on the Incarnation. Consider asking a friend or family member to do the same. Afterward, share your thoughts with one another.

Wednesday

Shepherds Interrupted
Luke 2:8-9; Psalm 86

The Savior of the world has arrived as a newborn baby, and he lies in a manger. After restoring the nativity to its first century context, we discover that Jesus' birth was very ordinary, nothing to indicate to those who witnessed his birth that royalty, the promised Jewish Messiah, has entered the room. Until…a knock at the door.

Who's there? A group of the Roman empire's ordinaries, some shepherds. What were these ordinary shepherds doing when they received news of the Savior's arrival and current location? Doing, of course, what they did night after night, out in the fields, watching over their sheep. The same sheep as last night and the night before. Under the same stars. Probably having the same conversations. Playing the same mind games to stay awake and alert. When suddenly, invading their ordinary, an angel appears, once again reminding us that God breaks into our lives as we go about the ordinary duties of life.

The shepherds highlight a sobering reality in our world—regardless of era, geographical location, spoken language, culture, available opportunities, or scientific advancements—communities create social structures. In the world's social structures, some people land on the top rung; others find themselves on the bottom rung. Each rung comes with a set of assumptions and privileges about themselves and others (some positive, others negative). Each rung grants a host of opportunities and limitations. In the first century, people classified shepherds among the lowliest class of people, uneducated and poor.

Of all the people to whom God could first announce the birth of Jesus—with whom God could begin spreading the good news—why would he choose the lowliest in society? Would not it have been more efficacious and impressive to notify the rich, the powerful, and/or the charismatic? After all, it is the rich and powerful who possess both platform and resources to advance an agenda. It is the charismatic among us who draw crowds and sway opinions. But Jesus came to restore not only individuals but entire communities back to their original vocation. Under Jesus' administration, all dividing walls have been demolished. Every identifying label into which this world squeezes a person falls away, bringing true equality and peace to communities.

Do you look at people based on the world's way of constructing communities or God's way of creating community?

Thursday

A Bold & Dangerous Declaration
Luke 2:10-14; Isaiah 52

Remember, whether a Jew or a Roman, a Greek or a Samaritan, a person living in the Roman Empire would know that when a herald brought *good news*, that news was always about a king. The proclamation either announced a future king's birth or a victory in battle, resulting in a change of administration. To rightly hear the angel's message to the shepherds, we need to listen like first century people living in the Roman Empire. (To review the meaning of *good news*, return to Thursday of week 1).

The herald angel's words assert a bold and dangerous claim. A new king has been born in Bethlehem, a king who will be for all people. Make no mistake. To allege that Jesus is king is to denounce Caesar as king. Then, in a demonstration of power and authority, authenticating the herald and its message, a regiment appears! A multitude of heavenly hosts is a regiment of warrior angels. And this regiment is not shouting "Hail, Caesar! Pax Romana!" but "Hail, Yahweh, the God of the Jews, who is bringing real peace for all men!"

Jesus is king. Kings rule kingdoms. Jesus' kingdom is called the kingdom of God. The Jews had been expectantly awaiting the coming of the kingdom of God. (See Monday of week 3.) During his earthly ministry, Jesus goes around preaching about, and bringing near, the kingdom of God. Jesus' coronation as king comes in the form of his crucifixion...the King with humble beginnings, in humility receives his crown.

What exactly is the kingdom of God? The kingdom of God is God's rule and reign intervening in the lives of people. The kingdom of God exists not as a place (such as heaven) but an event. When the kingdom of God comes near, wrongs are set right. This is the meaning behind the miracles Jesus performs during his earthly ministries. When Jesus intervenes in people's lives, bringing the kingdom of God: the blind see, the deaf hear, the lame walk, sinners are forgiven, the hungry eat, the naked are covered, the possessed and oppressed are freed, and the dead are resurrected. In Rome (in the kingdoms of this world), only some people, in varying degrees, experience "the good life" or any semblance of true peace. But when God's kingdom comes, all its citizens will know peace and all that makes for peace.

How (in what circumstances) have you experienced the kingdom of God?

Friday

Transformed and Compelled
Luke 2:14-20; Isaiah 6:1-8

As quickly as the angels come, they leave. The sky falls dark again but for its twinkling night-lights, the stars. Wide-eyed, mouths gaping, hearts palpitating, the ordinary shepherds look one to another in disbelief. The shepherds have just experienced the kingdom of God, God's rule and reign intervening in their lives. Society regards them as inferior, but God deems them worthy by the angelic visitation and the message they bring. Where the reality of living under Rome's oppressive rule looms like a dark cloud over every facet of life, the news of a new king brings hope that change and a real peace are coming.

Imagine. Suddenly, *it*—which could be seen for miles, towering over the wilderness of Bethlehem—catches the eye of one shepherd, and he blurts out in fear, "Do you think *he*, or one of his soldiers, saw the angels and heard the message?" *He* is Herod the Great (Rome's murderous, puppet-king of the Jews); *it* is Herod's palace (the third largest in the world, built high on a hill, its stature and position sending a message loud and clear about who sits enthroned as king, who holds power).

The shepherds hold their breath. Watching. Waiting. Quiet. Still.

Finally, excitement over the good news of great joy trumps any fear of Rome's power and presence as another shepherd blurts out, "We must go to Bethlehem and see for ourselves!" And so the ordinaries set off with their extraordinary news to find the utterly extraordinary disguised in the utterly ordinary.

The shepherds' compelling decision to go and see Jesus, and then tell others of the good news, brings us to another important truth about the kingdom of God. God's rule and reign are not purely spiritual and personal. An encounter with the kingdom of God transforms a person. This radical transformation spills out as words and deeds, transforming personal relationships and, potentially, entire communities. Put another way, an irresistible response to an encounter with the kingdom of God is to partner with God, working with him in the restoration of his good creation.

Have you allowed the shadow of the enemy to hold you back from going where God has called you? It is time to take your eyes off the enemy's facades and put them on the world's true king.

Saturday

Extraordinary Visitors
Matthew 2:1-12; Psalm 72

We position them, neatly, next to the shepherds and their sheep, numbering them one, two, three, camels alongside. But, according to Matthew, these magi do not belong at the manger scene. And just how many of them followed the star, making the journey to worship the king of the Jews, remains a mystery. Furthermore, by the time the magi arrive in Bethlehem, Jesus toddles on two feet, no longer an infant lying in a manger.

Imagine Bethlehem…a relatively insignificant small village absorbed into the territory of the great Roman Empire. Its inhabitants navigate life as peasants— their dwellings meager homes of stone, clumped together communal style. The census brought Joseph to Bethlehem, where his wife, Mary, gave birth to Jesus. Here, they have made their home. In villages like these, everybody knows everybody, including everybody's business. Surely Bethlehemites remember the night of Jesus' birth, drawing shepherds from the fields with good news of great joy, leaving everyone in wonder. Since then, things have normalized. Joseph, Mary, and Jesus have settled into the community. In all aspects, everything about Bethlehem and its inhabitants, including our trio, are utterly ordinary.

Until…cresting over the hill, an extraordinary sight appears—a caravan of magi from the east in search of a king, The magi wind through the dusty roads, making their way past the simple nondescript dwellings until they come to the home of Mary and Joseph. To toddler Jesus, these extraordinary visitors present extravagant gifts and worship the young king, who is clothed in, and surrounded by, the ordinary.

With Christmas, the climax of the Bible's story has begun. In and through Jesus (from his birth to his ascension), God's promises of salvation have come. This brings God's story to its climactic turning point. The redemption of the good world God created has budded. It will bloom in full at Jesus' return, which ushers in the final act of God's story. However, unlike other stories, this final act has no end, no curtain call, for *there will be no night there—no need for lamps or sun—for the Lord God will shine on them. And they will reign forever and ever* (Revelation 22:5, NLT).

Since Jesus' ascension, mankind has lived in Advent. Not the four-week prelude to Christmas, but the second Advent, Jesus' return. Are you living an Advent life —living in a state of constant expectation, and anticipation of Jesus' return? What does it look like to live an Advent life?

Bibliography

Bailey, Kenneth E. *Jesus Through Middle Eastern Eyes*. Downers Grove: InterVaristy Press, 2008. Print.

Brock, Darrell L. *Baker Exegetical Commentary on the New Testament: Luke 1:1-9:50*. Grand Rapids: Baker Academic, 1994. Print.

Croteau, David A. *Urban Legends of the New Testament: 40 Common Misconceptions*. Nashville: B&H Publishing Group, 2015. Print.

Carter, Warren. *The Roman Empire and the New Testament*. Nashville: Abingdon Press, 1995. Print.

Eldredge, John. *Beautiful Outlaw*. New York: FaithWords, 2011. Print.

Holy Bible. New Living Translation. Tyndale House, 2005.

Keener, Craig S. *The IVP Background Commentary New Testament*. Downers Grove: InterVarsity Press, 1993. Print.

---. *The IVP Background Commentary Old Testament*. Downers Grove: InterVaristy Press, 1993. Print.

Morphew, Derek. *Breakthrough: Discovering the Kingdom*. Cape Town: Vineyard International Publishing, 1991. Print.

Richards, F. Randolph and Brandon J O'Brien. *Misreading Scripture through Western Eyes*. Downers Grove: IVP Academic, 2012. Print.

Ryken, Leland, Jim Wilhoit, and Tremper Longman. *Dictionary of Biblical Imagery*. Downers Grove: IVP Academic, 1998. Print.

Spangler, Ann, and Lois Tverberg. *Sitting at the Feet of Rabbi Jesus*. Grand Rapids: Zondervan, 2009. eBook.

Ware, Timothy. *The Orthodox Church*. Great Britain: Penguin Random House, 1963. Print

Warren, Monica Napoli. *Exploring the Kingdom of God Together: A Devotional Journey for Small Groups*. Create Space, 2018. Print.

Wright, N.T. "Gospel and Theology in Galatians," *N.T. Wright Page*, Retrieved June 13, 2011.http://ntwrightpage.com/Wright_Gospel_Theology_Galatians.pdf

---. *How God Became King*. New York: Harper Collins, 2012. Print.

---. *Simply Jesus*. New York: Harper Collins, 2011. Print.

---. *The Day the Revolution Began*. New York: Harper Collins, 2016. Kindle Edition.

Zahnd, Brian. *Beauty Will Save the World: Rediscovering the Allure and Mystery of Christianity*. Lake Mary: Charisma House, 2012. Print.

Acknowledgments

Like any other work, this one bears the fingerprints of many hands and hearts, without which this project would not even exist. Each project I have done has been a labor of love—freely I have been given, freely I give. Likewise, those who lend their God-given gifts and expertise to each project do so as a gift. Every person listed below is family, some ordained by God through blood and others joined by his kingdom. I deeply love and greatly appreciate each of these unique image-bearing humans.

Thank You...

Sarah Brenner for tirelessly reading and rereading and marking and rewording each devotion; for setting an example of faithful living in every season; and being a bottomless reservoir of love, encouragement, and enthusiasm.

Nancy Ash for carefully editing each devotion and for being a safe place to wrestle with doctrine and theology.

Evelyn Napoli (better known to me as "Mom") for boldly taking a vision in your head, and an idea I had in my heart, and painting it in order to create this devotional's cover. Life is more fun with you living next door!

Claude for always encouraging me to fly while faithfully holding the rope to keep me grounded; for being willing to grow and learn and change together. Doing life with you is one among my greatest joys and privileges.

About Monica Napoli Warren

Perpetual student. Mediocre triathlete. Lousy cook. Devoted wife to one very patient man. Proud mom of two. Mimi to one. Lives in Mobile, Alabama. Reads a lot about Jesus. Goes around speaking of Jesus. Hopes she is growing more into Jesus' likeness.

Monica fell in love with teaching Bible studies in her early twenties while serving as a Young Life leader during college. Over the past thirty years, she has led women's ministry, taught and written material for countless Bible studies and Sunday school classes, and spoken at numerous events and conferences. Monica earned her Master of Theological Studies at Southwestern Baptist Theological Seminary—admittedly an odd choice among seminaries for a woman who has always worshiped in the Anglican tradition, but the perfect opportunity for growing in biblical understanding outside her echo chamber.

Printed in Great Britain
by Amazon